Words for Things Left Unsaid

Words for Things Left Unsaid

Poems by

Corie Rosen

Cover design by Shay Culligan

ISBN: 978-1-950462-81-0

Kelsay Books Inc.

kelsaybooks.com

502 S 1040 E, A119
American Fork,Utah 84003

With love, to Jeffrey, my heart

And with thanks to Ishmael Reed, my teacher

Acknowledgments

Triggerfish Critical Review: "Dinosaur Bones"

Konch: "An Orange Flower Called Grace," "Instructions for Forgetting," "The World According to Garp," "Of Eros and Dust"

34ᵗʰ Parallel: "This Above All Else"

Contents

Crossroad

With you now,
I arrive at the place where
once reached
I must, or at least, have already begun
to say the things I'd promised
I'd keep sealed inside myself.

Words that rise from the dust-rimmed pavement,
flotsam that drifts up from the curbside,
words meant to be held beneath the closed jar's lid.

It is too soon to say how
I loved you, love you, love you,
will love you all over again
in whatever that word's
(strained) future tense may be.

But, as I think I've already mentioned,
I'm not going to say this.
Anyway, it is too soon for those sorts of declarations.

Yet, here we are, walking through the night
hand in hand, already arrived on this corner
and standing now, so still together
there are all these things that must be said.

The Thousandth Word for Snow

The time I first saw cottonwood—
so easily mistaken for a dream
(or at least a dream state)
I woke and stepped out of the tent
into a swirling summer flurry.

It was as if a winter slush
had sliced across the warmth of the valley.
Those pale blossoms
against the blue
were as out of place as I was
(let's be honest)
on the rocky ladder
of the high mountainside.

Each puff descended in its rhythm,
a pulsing I could keep up with as, in time,
each one trailed as if tracing
an individual, roped column of light.

Now, in the street, I step into puddles of curled cotton
open my mouth to catch one, to tongue the bloom.
I swallow back the animal fur,
feel it harsh against my throat, jagged,
catch my breath when you come running,
when I recognize the question in your eyes.

Your face, always a surprise,
your mouth, pink as the season,
your tongue flicking the shape of an answer,
a word that only I can say or know.
There, again, this secret language, phrases we hold between us,
unspeakable as the many names for that summer snow.

This bridal flurry, sudden as your presence,
(only, your face—it's imagined)
and the cottonwood blooms, I cannot name them
cannot say all the words that I have yet to read or fathom
cannot follow the climb,
of the other notes
you might use to describe them.

They, too, are distant bodies raining, voiceless
into this dazzle, into this fury,
into this pale sheet of thin morning rain.

Life from Bone

All day long, the sofa wrestles daylight,
spilling it: toss, grab; grab, toss.

The fabric is a mirror in a painted frame
that reflects the room back and doubles
the garish gleam of this place called home.

A sofa, after all, is only an object.
It cannot decide where the light should wander,
or where it should remain.
And so the gray sofa sits, passive and clasping.
Its threads have a sheen (fixed, but optimistic).
It is waiting for someone else to come along
and tell it what it means.

Alone, I lean over its gray back, reach to open the window.
I turn with force the old, slow crank.
Outside, the afternoon begins to settle.
In the yard, the breeze mumbles through the piles of dry leaves.

Even here, where you never were,
the air has learned the syllables of your absence.
Somehow, I have taught this room to hum
the music of your name.

Later, I work slowly, preparing chicken.
It is obscene, this—
slipping skin from flesh, pulling life from bone,
all hope truant.
My hands move through this air that is your lack.

I thought I was finished with this sad world.
I thought I was home at last, preparing chicken.
I work, and remember the lines of your body:
neck, feet, hips, your sideways smile.

Maybe, where you sit in your office, or on your own sofa,
with others, or even alone (maybe)
you imagine the gold light of this kitchen,
the smell of chicken roasting
expertly, murderously
(as it is just now).

Outside, the trees in my yard are awake to their fall burning.
Palms open, they cast down their leaves like lost lovers' hands.
Toss all you want, I say.
It won't help you.
Though the trees, conscious of their own mortality,
decline to hear what I have to say.

The trees know even less than the sofa.
They do not realize
the way a room can hold your scent
(even if you've never been here)
the way the fog traces your name
long after you have gone.

/Bind/ *verb,* meaning to secure or fasten

A voice that death cannot erase,
the memory is a vine binding my wrists, even in its shadow
it ties my arms, my ankles, and my legs
links the little islands of my breaths with its full-leafed length.

He and I both know grosgrain traps just as easily as plain ribbon.

Still, I shiver at the familiar chafe,
the tightening of the wrap,
the breath behind the words,
unspoken and unsaid.

There is, in the pull of this vine,
a feeling like something unwritten,
law that is as yet unknown,
love like another country.
The actions of the body,
inescapable and repeating,
you and then me and you and you and me again.
Bodies touching, one and then two,
over and over,
a tessellation in flesh, in time, in thought and words.

Love like breath we do not will.
Love like pictures of unknown places.
Love like the myth of man
who tells himself
there is moral weight
in what he does or does not do,
who does not know how he lies to himself when he says
there is a pattern in his choosing.

I had forgotten what it was like
to be wrapped like this,
held in place by this green length
by these unread vowels
by this ecstatic sorrow
by these two hidden hearts that,
once set together, bind.

Dinosaur Bones

My niece, who is three
is twirling in a sparkly dress, her favorite Hello Kitty gown.
She moves, jerking, across the brown expanse of the kitchen.
I think she is probably the same age as your daughter,
though it has been many years since I have seen you
and I do not know for sure.
She is blonde and holds a book about
how dinosaurs clean their rooms.
Later, I will read it to her on the sofa while she squirms—
a little child in a large bed,
still and new and smooth, that warm little body,
curling with innocence, with expectation and heat.

On campus, there was a bright atrium,
green windows and walls like white columns.
At the pale, high, center, the preserved skeleton of
a Tyrannosaurus Rex.
I remember how the predator's hull hung
shuddering from the ceiling
taking up all the air and light, this dead thing,
still powerful at the center of the room.

I used to visit that tall body
though I was not a science student
and the hall was a long way
from the converted church where I studied dance.
That ancient skeleton held a memory of a memory,
the bloody taste my own evolution had buried,
a memory of a time
before man and daylight mammals
were mud-colored and inventive (the way that they are now).
It was only this: a vast arc of raw hunger,
a high necked form of predatory leg and bone.

At school, I'd studied you also.
The winding pattern of the cream you swirled into your coffee,
the dirty leaf smell of your late-night breath.
A scientist might have told me how electrons spilled
from the tips of your fingers,
how it was particles of you that made
the charge across my skin.

Then there were the soft-aired afternoons when I slipped silently
across campus
searching for you in the smell of the wet grass,
in the hum of the creek,
in the damp stretch of afternoon pavement,
on those rainy afternoons when I went hunting dinosaur bones.

Another Country

Can we two live apart,
but (as in prior centuries' poems)
meet beneath a single star's light?
If the moment and the line allow,
that glinting star is ours.

Caught, held, the night a firefly
trapped in the palm of a cloudless evening,
our little star beams back on itself
traversing, as it does,
the plains of history, physics, space, and language.

Here now, my darkened room
is lit by the orange pulse of the street light
scented by my cheap candles,
by the dust of the slowly bluing sky.
You are with me, in your way,
neither smiling nor breathing,
a memory caught in the space between
darkness and morning,
captive in the corridor
between midnight and new light.

Yes, even now,
as you sleep in another house, in another bedroom,
in a town so high and strange that I cannot
begin to speak or reach it,
a city that seems to exist beneath
another star's slow gleaming light
another place, another name, another country,
words that form the language of
a real and different life.

There, your chest heaves in sleep,
another body warms and curls beside you.
Though you are with me, here, now,
I close my eyes and see the two of you together,
breathing beneath that star that once seemed our only
syllable, now stilled and high,
casting its ancient spark in its unknown language,
beaming down and down with its warm, familial light.

An Orange Flower Called Grace

There was the afternoon when I came home
and found you on the stoop
of the old Victorian where, upstairs,
I rented a room with dark blue curtains.

The house was a peach whisper in green overgrowth,
painted steps, peeling trim along the siding.
Where you sat, or just below where you sat,
the lawn rose, uncut and untended.
You were like that grass then,
pitched high and rustling,
triumphant, knowing you'd done well
in the breezy afternoon light.

In your hand, a flower,
orange—
one I did not know the name of.
Though the smooth, furred petals
made me want to know.

You held it tight,
this unnamed thing,
a whole life wrapped up in brown paper
tied with a length of white ribbon,
knotted at the flower's throat.

I remember:
the way your gaze turned,
the way you leaned forward when you saw me walking.
The way that I came toward you, and
like your gaze,
your whole body curved upward.

Maybe it was a gerbera or a lily,
a delphinium,
or a phlox,
Maybe it was something in-between,
Some laboratory creation,
dreamed up by a secret scientist
whose name no one will ever tell.

I remember how I hurried up the steps,
wanting to arrive, to reach you,
already inside the moment
when you would stand and
hold out the unnamed flower,
your eyes fixed on the slice of air
the line between us
the line between
anger and forgiveness,
(between where we once were
and where you wished we'd stood).

I remember the blue air of that day,
the way the paint flecks dangling from the siding
held their breath in stillness
when you handed me the nameless thing.
My fingers stretched to reach it,
to grasp the line,
to hold the moment when
I would know the word to name the orange petals,
when, in the echo of that sound,
our hands would finally meet.

Seen Only Once

Why is it that there are those who
I see everyday,
yet they leave no feeling in me?
But you,
seen only once
(a sly smile over a too-small table)
with you there is not only memory
but a sense of change?

How (and why) did you alter me,
and so quickly?
There was the brush of a hand
after dinner
the low hum of the summer water
the river running too high.
We went to look up at the Ferris wheel
lit up on the narrow bankside.
A spark of danger (even then),
creases around your eyes
lines I had not seen before that.

We stood on one side of the tracks,
fingers quickly closed and
pulled back in the darkness.
It was only a single touch,
a little instance,
little insistence,
and now I wake to the thought of it each morning.
You and you and you,
as my eyes flicker open.
You and you and you,
and somehow I am different,

even as I sleep in the same bed in the same house,
even as I wear the same shirt,
the same perfume,
even as I dress to meet the day.

Maybe you are only a feeling.
A prickling that spreads
along the backs of my legs and spinal column.
You and you and you.
The bright flash at our touching
the backs of two hands brushing
on that bank, in that stillness, out there in the wordless dark.

Your forgotten scent,
your tall heat next to my body.
The way that night, for just that moment,
I'd wanted to let you hold my hand in your hand,
to let it stay closed there
in the silent darkness
to stand still on that bank together
for an unmeasured length of time.

Instructions for Forgetting

Let us not attempt
the tangles and twists of the body,
the acrobatics that our young shapes once performed.
Let us not reach, warm-palmed, toward the past,
with its rose-lipped letters.
Let us not mourn the gray stones
whose names we once thought
we'd be excused from learning how to say.

Lost now, the sharpness of our features,
shifted in the millions of moments since we were last seen.
Let us be new, then,
here, now
ageless (or almost)
only our two tanned bodies
and the cold of the air conditioner,
quiet now
in the still air of this room.

Familiar as we can be
here, again as though at first
the room chilly and indifferent.
Draped windows that ease onto a view of buildings and sky.
High up places, unknown to us,
they range like ghosts around us,
hungry all the time,
showing their teeth to the passerby.

Look West, oh please, look West—
Oh, please. (Come on, just do it.)
West to the shoreline,
to the sun,
to the memory of what each of us was
in the moment we were last seen.

We were ever only ourselves,
youth and beauty we did not know
how to speak or look at.
And so we held our breath
anticipating tomorrows,
the years ahead imagined and imperfect,
though they were always only happening now.

Then, this small white room was unthinkable,
unknown to us.
Though perhaps it was as inevitable,
as the movement of waves along the sea
that wide, salted, ancient, graveyard
over whose depths you'd departed
on that morning when
you were first flown
first gone and lost to me.

Of Eros and Dust

The blue winter stars
believed they'd dreamt
the black bed of the sky
in which they gathered.
Like scattered drops of snow, they lay,
sheltering their light (and their hubris)
in the dry grasses below.

Tonight, as I walk,
the roads and hillsides double and redouble,
tense with the blue light
of the high mountain sky.

These are the stars who know
how a moment comes on—quick and sudden
a darkling sun
a burst
a break
a tear
in the sapphire quiet of the night.
There, too, overhead, are the stars that cover up the gravesites.
The stony curves beneath which the airless sleepers lie.
Tonight their plots are still, silver-dipped and dreamless
silent in the rustling of the leaves,
in the heaving of our feet as we pass.

They have no voice, but lie
in shared memory
in the garden
it is hard to believe that they once rose and breathed,
walked this path exactly, or more exactly, perhaps, than we did
touched their feet to the cool earth
just as we are doing now.

This Above All Else

This above all else:
Write nothing pastoral.
Do not celebrate the seasons.
Do not clasp hands with time.
Do not write about love.
(Whatever you do, please don't do that.)

This above all else:
No lines about fields and gardens.
There are people screaming in the streets and
it's not the nineteenth century after all.

This above all else:
No more dreamy eyes turned cloudward.
No more of this lover's business.
No more stars winking in unselfconscious delight.

This above all else:
The slithering line of the freeway.
The smog lung of this city.
The men who cry "science is a hoax"
while we (by which I mean you and I)
busy ourselves
trying urgently not to love.

This above all else:
The cries of "it was always happening."
The boys who watched hope slip from its sockets.
The girls who turned their eyes skyward
as we all did, once, faces tilted upward
to try to forget how to welcome
the sweet, soft breath of night.

Waking Early

There is a feeling like white jasmine
scented and familiar,
pale, though full,
and at the same time
a surprise.

The way that it swells like heat expanding in the body.
The way that it comes on after waking
and bends the chest.

It is a feeling nearly—or precisely—indistinguishable from
heartbreak.
A love that feels close to (or identical to) pain.

This, then, is late summer jasmine,
a surprise that is also suffering,
white, scented, familiar as childhood,
a sweetness that signals the season's end,
a pale loss flowering with the plants that open their eyes at dawn.

Here, in these white sheets,
you lie next to me, dreaming,
I don't want to move or breathe,
don't want to flex my little finger,
don't want to unwrap my hand, my mind,
don't want to unbind this language
from where your body and mine are almost (or nearly) an ours.

It seems, for a moment, possible, to remain here always,
suspended by the scent of jasmine
our bodies wound into one another,
an ours, already touching,
our minds unfurling slowly
dreaming, or thinking summer thoughts only,
curled inside this heat and light,
ignorant of the fall.

A Definition, in the End

In the kitchen she said, that's it. We're through—finished.
He said, life is not a movie. Even if you'd like it to be.
He said, this is our story. There is no neat ending.
Go on, then, she said. I dare you.
Go, go on. Please just do it.
He said, the way you talk about it.
There's the trouble.
She said, I'm sorry. I'm so sorry.
She said, all my life I'd thought
"violence" was just another word for love.

The World According to Garp

At first it had been simple.
Eyes across the theater—
the haystack smell
of two young actors' breaths,
lingering in the rafters.

Later, we walked home in the twilight.
"Notice Magic,"
letters somebody had scrawled into the wet cement
who knew how many years before.

It was autumn then, fall in California,
orange haloes made circles around the streetlamps,
and the pavement was smooth,
damp with rain the whole way through.

Memories of other lovers' dewy mornings
were stored in the sidewalk cracks beneath us,
they sighed as we disturbed them
with the pounding of our feet.
I remember your dark hair, too long,
the way it looked black in the lamplight.

A metal smell, salt-water scent from the Pacific.
The brine of youth, of evening, bright,
like the promise of the future,
lay suspended in the fog that rose
over the half-stilled bay.
Around us, the cool air was half invitation, half warning
the same scent that all our lives
had marked that place, that rain.

In your face, I saw questions—yours or mine—I wasn't certain.
Knowing, not knowing,
then knowing and not knowing again.
We were only that—young, scared, and uncertain,
caught out in the heart's vast late-night rain.

Still, our fingers made swirls through the hungry darkness
and, for all our doubts, we still leaned forward
found a way to touch palm to palm, skin to skin.

Then, real life again, standing in your doorway.
The knob against your hand a cold mound of uncertain silver.
You turned it and the painted door swung back,
the night expanded, made an orange flare
in the thick of the sky's bruise.

Later, there would be the final fight.
Hot afternoon, smoggy sun, your Los Angeles apartment.
The low and hateful sprawl of the blue Murphy bed.
Past the windows, the hills cupped polluted daylight,
as though it were something precious and not
the sign of the End of Times.
In spite of the blinds, the acid light screamed in, yellow,
managed to choke and press itself into the room.

Now, when I think of that day,
I cannot always recall your gestures,
cannot always see your blue-black hair,
or conjure the slant of your smile,
cannot remember the words of the book whose pages,
with their clean smell of bookstore ink
(an apology, newly purchased)
would be the last gift you ever gave.

If I Lost You (Have I Lost You?)

If you fell away from me
the way the red leaves fall in autumn
from their places on the maple,
I'd let you go.
If you tucked yourself up dark and small
stowed inside of one of the attic's many forgotten boxes,
I'd let you be.
If you stripped bare on the damp lip of the shoreline,
threw your body into the salt sting of the breakers,
I would not lose myself
swimming after you.

If I lost you to the sea, the air, the sky,
the changing of the seasons,
if you went away from me
and told me not to follow
I would not hold you in my palm,
and try to close my fingers
would not try to close my heart
around the folded loss.

At night, I would not think of you,
would not curl into your memory,
would not close my arms
around the imaginary pulse
of my laundered bedsheets.

If you turned from me,
the way the sun turns from life
on the grayest mornings,
if you looked past me for so long
I wondered if I'd ever really found you,
if you did any of these things
I wouldn't scream or cry or mourn you,
because I once would have spoken

in the words of our shared language
each phrase an earring, a loose diamond,
each line its own small precious object,
each sound its own tiny, bright and perfect thing.

A Season without Language

Now I see that words are just pale hollows
thin-leafed and flimsy
their shapes spilled
like the points of forgotten, black-eyed stars.

Nothing is said between
the arms of two people
trying to reach one another
(because their lives depended on it,
or because they were only human,
or because they could not help it,
or, later,
for what felt like no reason at all).

These words are only white ash, yours and mine, truly.
Unless they give life to: the pattern of the seasons,
gold and green fronds glimmering,
the crusted bits of ice clinging at the edge of a white branch.
Or else they walk you down the street,
spying on your neighbors,
faces whose lips tell silent stories
as they tense and blue against the cold.

Or perhaps they tell of all the grave eyes now shuttered,
of last, hungry glances toward other summers' suns.
Always, the words are ash.
Always the blue eyes are gone black with understanding
of the bleached and wordless season—
so many possible sounds, and yet no way to name it,
this loneliness, this separation,
this time apart from language,

the you of me and the me of you,
inside our separate bodies,
the abandoned days,
the separate skins,
the thing that is still to come.

Words for Things Unsaid

Today I am full of sorrow,
(or is it regret, or maybe longing?)
Regardless, I will not write to tell you
how I sat in my kitchen
listening to the footsteps of the women cleaning
the titters of the squirrels along the fences
the voices of the men who are at work
across the street,
building a house.

A new house and a good house,
large enough for a single, happy family.
The men are chatting and laughing.
I can hear them (not their words, but the songs inside their voices).
Maybe as they talk, they are thinking of the children
the two or three or four, who will live inside those walls.
Which of the men are the ones who laugh as they lean down,
which are the ones who force a smile
which are the ones who tense and heave
as they brace the high wood frame?
I wonder which of those men might feel (perhaps) as I do—
rent, not as in charged, but as in a length of shredded silk.
The white puff of the fabric,
stowed out of sight like sickness,
torn in slender, jagged pieces,
not to be seen.

Today, in my kitchen
there is only the sink full of unwashed dishes
and these tatters, hidden,
tears for which no one has yet invented a machine.

Would I still ache if, all those years ago, I had told you?
said the one thing I did not have words for then?
If I'd run my hands over the dirty floorboards,
if, just for a moment, I'd rested my head on your shoulder
if I'd found a word to name that silk
to mark its width and length?

What might have happened if,
even as recently as yesterday morning,
I had said:
that yours is the only face,
yours the only shadow,
yours the only voice,
yours the only words,
the only language,
your line the only echo on this hard, round, wild planet,
and that the shelter of your breath,
of your body,
of your memory,
of your presence,
is the only only house, the only home
my heart has ever known.

About the Author

Corie Rosen is a fiction writer, poet, and arts educator. Her poetry and short fiction have been anthologized, featured on NPR, and are regularly included in high school and college curricula. Her writing has appeared in award-winning magazines, including *Arts & Letters, Crab Creek Review, Juked, Konch,* and *Two Cities Review,* among many other places.

She has been a finalist for the Katherine Anne Porter Prize and for the Raymond Carver Short Story Prize. In 2017, her work was nominated for the Pushcart Prize.

She has taught at University of California, Los Angeles, at Arizona State University, and at the University of Colorado, Boulder. She lives in Denver with her husband and young daughter, where she is a member of the Lighthouse Writers Workshop.

www.ingramcontent.com/pod-product-compliance
Lightning Source LLC
Chambersburg PA
CBHW031154090426
42738CB00008B/1336